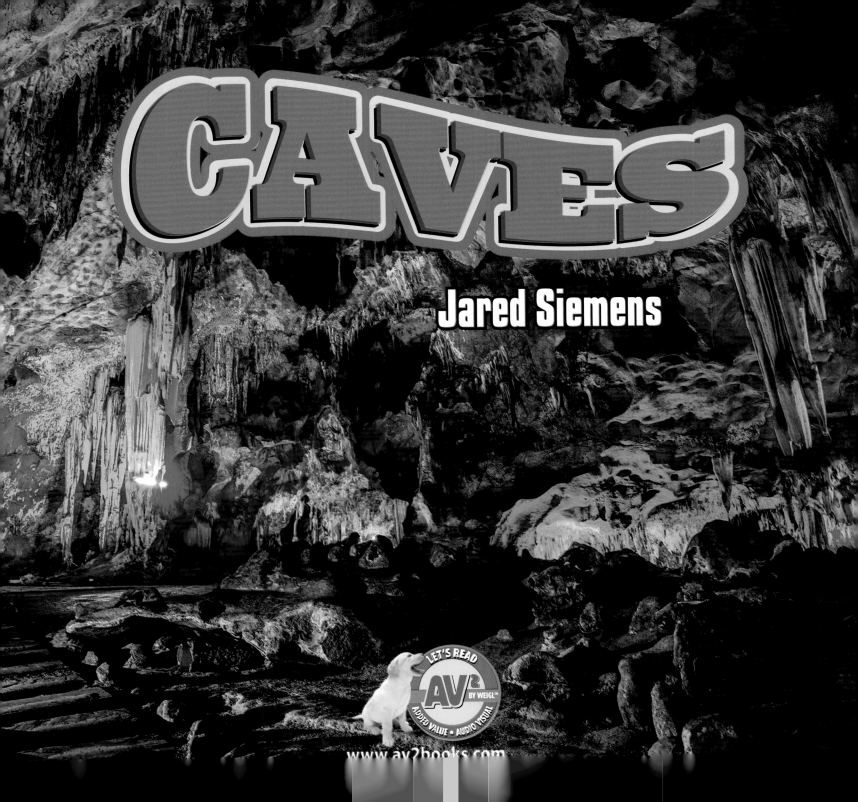

CAVES

Jared Siemens

LET'S READ
AV2 BY WEIGL
ADDED VALUE • AUDIO VISUAL
www.av2books.com

LET'S READ
AV²
BY WEIGL™
ADDED VALUE • AUDIO VISUAL

Go to **www.av2books.com,**
and enter this book's
unique code.

BOOK CODE

Y 5 9 6 4 7 8

AV² by Weigl brings you media
enhanced books that support
active learning.

AV² provides enriched content that supplements and complements this book. Weigl's AV² books strive to create inspired learning and engage young minds in a total learning experience.

Your AV² Media Enhanced books come alive with...

Audio
Listen to sections of
the book read aloud.

Video
Watch informative
video clips.

Embedded Weblinks
Gain additional information
for research.

Try This!
Complete activities and
hands-on experiments.

Key Words
Study vocabulary, and
complete a matching
word activity.

Quizzes
Test your knowledge.

Slide Show
View images and
captions, and prepare
a presentation.

... and much, much more!

Published by AV² by Weigl
350 5th Avenue, 59th Floor New York, NY 10118
Website: www.av2books.com

Library of Congress Control Number: 2015956073

ISBN 978-1-4896-4165-6 (hardcover)
ISBN 978-1-4896-4166-3 (softcover)
ISBN 978-1-4896-4167-0 (single-user eBook)
ISBN 978-1-4896-4168-7 (multi-user eBook)

Printed in the United States of America in Brainerd, Minnesota
1 2 3 4 5 6 7 8 9 0 19 18 17 16 15

112015   Project Coordinator: Jared Siemens
111315   Design: Mandy Christiansen

The publisher acknowledges Alamy, Getty Images, Corbis Images, and iStock as the primary image suppliers for this title.
Pg. 12 image (Pilea cavernicola) courtesy Alex Monro

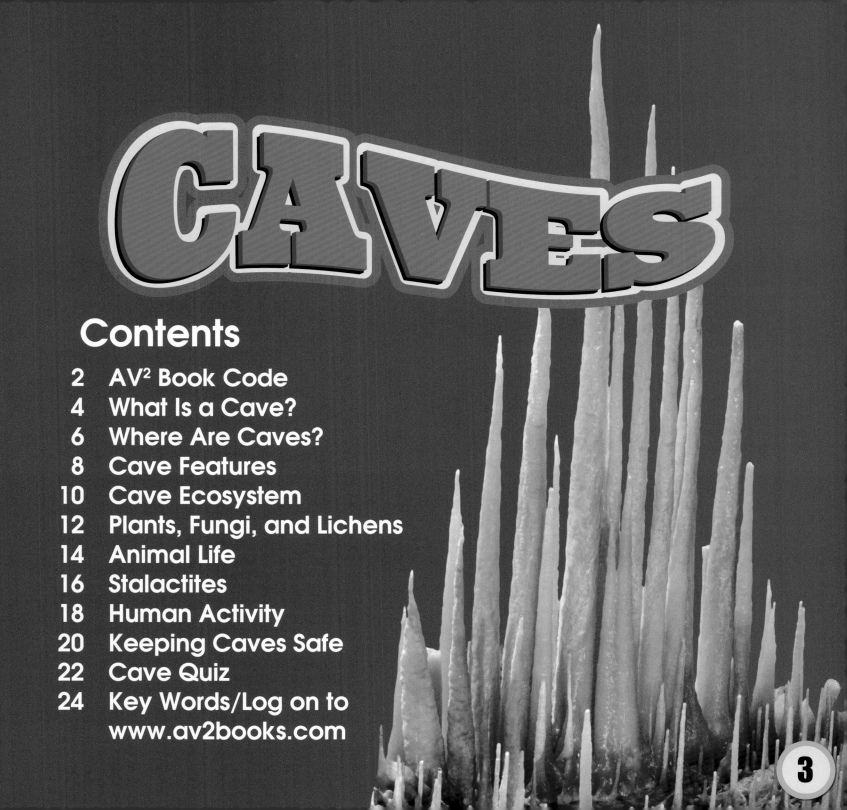

CAVES

Contents

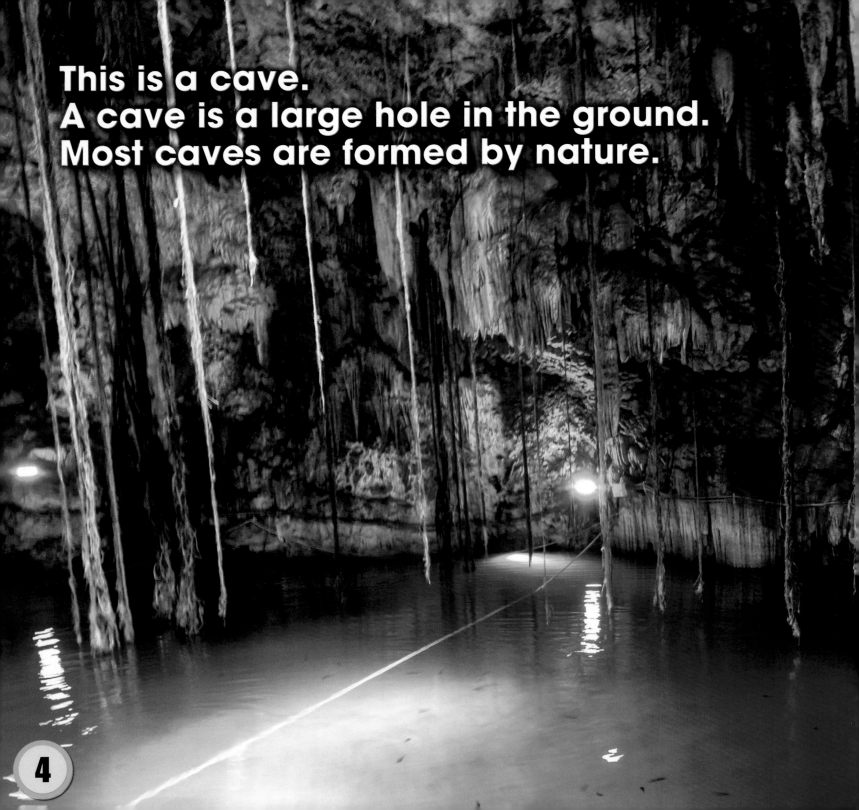

This is a cave.
A cave is a large hole in the ground.
Most caves are formed by nature.

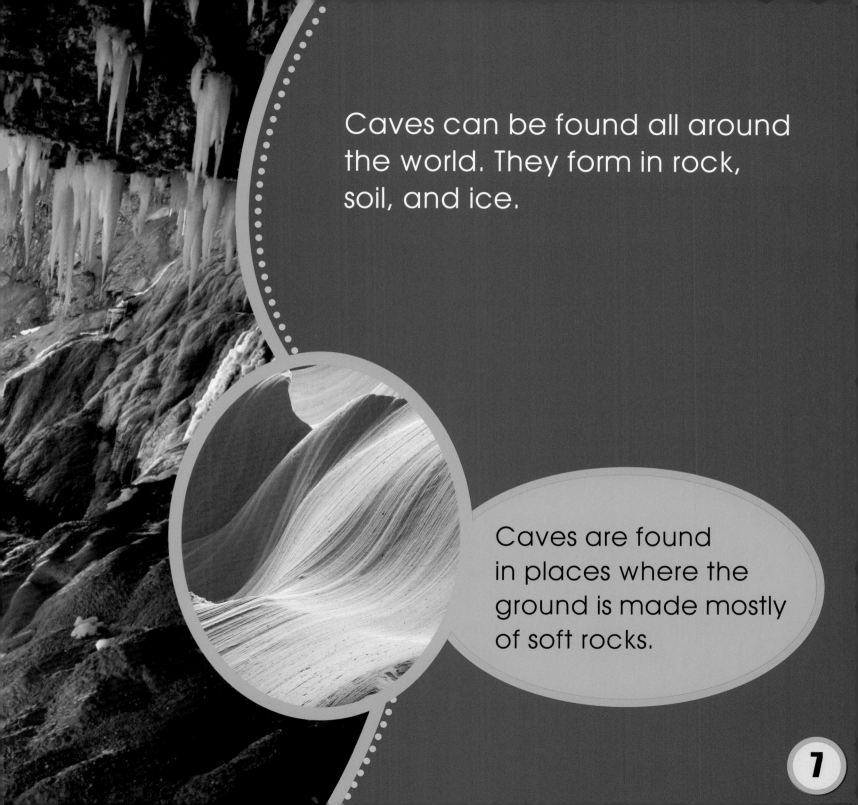

Caves can be found all around the world. They form in rock, soil, and ice.

Caves are found in places where the ground is made mostly of soft rocks.

Wind and water carve large holes and tunnels in the ground. It takes many years for wind and water to wear away rock.

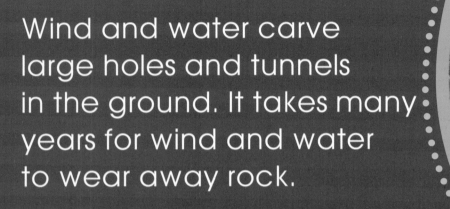

Mammoth Cave in Kentucky has more than 400 miles (644 kilometers) of tunnels.

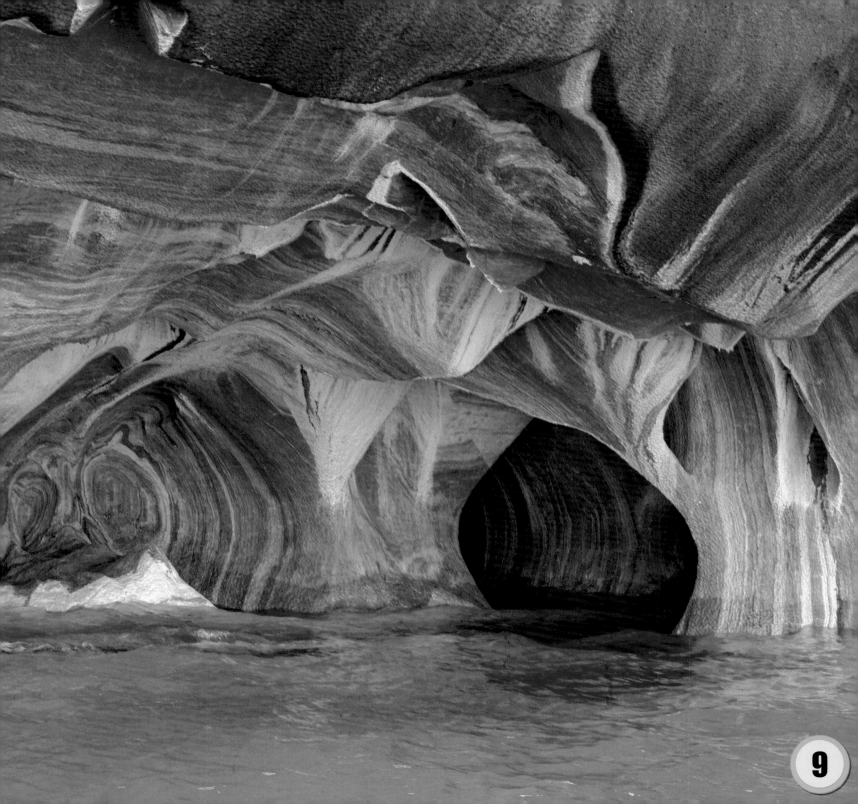

Eastern phoebes make nests along cave walls.

Fungi recycle plant and animal waste.

Copperhead snakes feed on other cave animals.

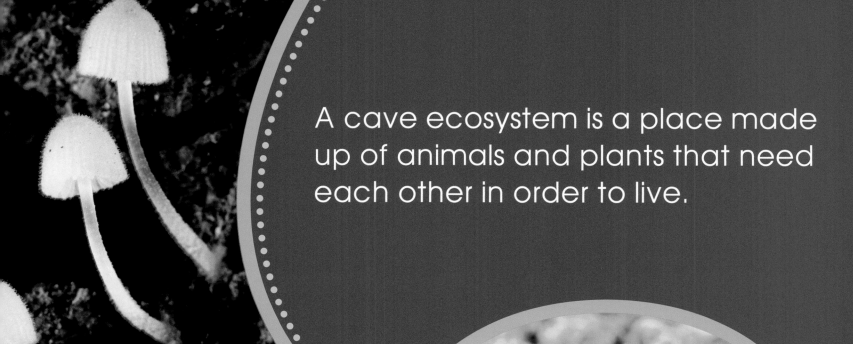

A cave ecosystem is a place made up of animals and plants that need each other in order to live.

Beetles feed on cricket eggs.

Amazonian giant centipedes hunt bats in caves.

Plants, fungi, and lichens all live in caves. They are an important part of a cave ecosystem.

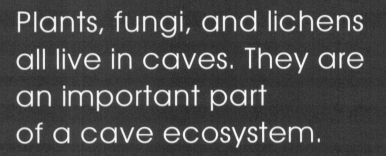

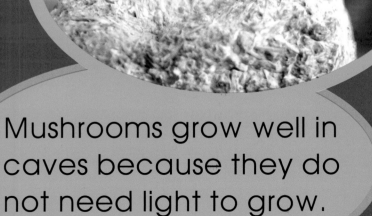

Mushrooms grow well in caves because they do not need light to grow.

Mosses have root-like parts that help them grow on rocks.

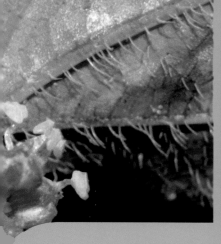

Cave nettles can grow and flower with very little light.

Ferns grow in the shade of cave openings.

Lichens provide a home for insects.

Many different animals make
their homes in caves.

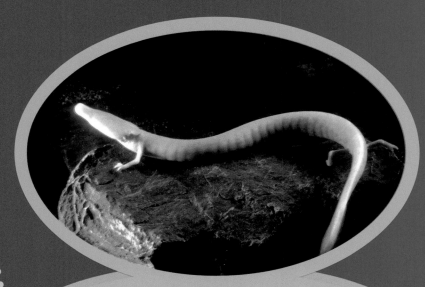

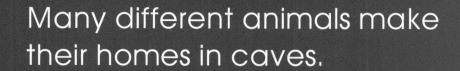

Pack rats use smell
to find their nests
in dark caves.

Olms can live up to
10 years without food.

Caves are full of rocks. Some cave rocks hang like icicles. These rocks are called stalactites.

The Jeita Grotto in Lebanon has the world's longest stalactite. It is 27 feet (8.2 meters) long.

Miners dig for gold and silver in caves. This digging can hurt the caves and the animals that live there.

THIS CAVE IS PROTECTED BY VIRGINIA STATE LAW

Some states make laws to keep caves and cave animals safe.

Scientists go into caves to learn more about the plants and animals there. They need special tools to get in and out of caves.

People who visit caves should not take anything or leave anything behind.

Cave Quiz

See what you have learned about cave ecosystems.

Find these cave animals and plants in the book. What are their names?

KEY WORDS

Research has shown that as much as 65 percent of all written material published in English is made up of 300 words. These 300 words cannot be taught using pictures or learned by sounding them out. They must be recognized by sight. This book contains 88 common sight words to help young readers improve their reading fluency and comprehension. This book also teaches young readers several important content words, such as proper nouns. These words are paired with pictures to aid in learning and improve understanding.

Page	Sight Words First Appearance
4	a, are, by, in, is, large, most, the, this
7	all, and, around, be, can, found, made, of, places, they, where, world
8	away, for, has, more, it, many, miles, takes, than, to, water, years
10	along, animals, make, on, other, plant
11	each, live, need, that, up
12	an, because, do, grow, have, help, important, light, not, part, them, well
13	home, little, very, with
14	down, find, food, from, often
15	different, their, use, without
16	feet, like, long, some, these
19	keep, states, there
20	about, get, go, into, learn, leave, or, out, people, should, who

Page	Content Words First Appearance
4	cave, ground, hole, nature
7	ice, rock, soil
8	Kentucky, Mammoth Cave, tunnels, wind
10	fungi, nests, phoebes, snakes, walls, waste
11	bats, beetles, centipedes, cricket, ecosystem, eggs
12	lichens, mosses, mushrooms
13	ferns, insects, nettles, openings, shade
14	bears, cavefish, ceilings, winter
15	olms, rats
16	icicles, Jeita Grotto, Lebanon, stalactites
19	gold, laws, miners, silver
20	scientists, tools